Dear Parent:

Do you want to spark your child's creativity? Do you want your child to become a confident writer? Road to Writing can help.

Road to Writing is a unique creative writing program that gives even the youngest writers a chance to express themselves. Featuring five distinct levels, or Miles, the Road to Writing program accompanies children from their first attempts at writing to comfortably writing on their own.

A Creative Start
For children who "write" stories by drawing pictures
• easy picture prompts • familiar subjects • places to draw

Creative Writing With Help
For children who write easy words with help
• detailed picture prompts • places to draw and label

Creative Writing On Your Own
For children who write simple sentences on their own
• basic story starters • popular topics • places to write

First Journals
For children who are comfortable writing short paragraphs
• more complex story starters • space for free writing

Journals
For children who want to try different kinds of writing
• cues for poems, jokes, stories • brainstorming pages

There's no need to hurry through the Miles. Road to Writing is designed without age or grade levels. Children can progress at their own speed, developing confidence and pride in their writing ability along the way.

Road to Writing—"write" from the start!

Look for these Road to Writing books

Mile 1

Cool School
Super Me!

Mile 2

Boo!
Road Trip

Mile 3

Monkey Business
Sports Shorts

Tips for Using this Book

- Help your child read each page. Then let your child draw or write a response—right in the book!

- Don't worry—there are no "right" or "wrong" answers. This book is a place for your child to be creative.

- Remind your child to write at his or her own pace. There's no rush!

- Encourage your child with plenty of praise.

Pencils, pens, and crayons are all suitable for use in this book. Markers are not recommended.

A GOLDEN BOOK • New York
Golden Books Publishing Company, Inc. New York, New York 10106

ISBN: 0-307-45403-7 A MCMXCIX

Road Trip

by Sarah Albee and

____

(your name)

illustrated by
Liisa Chauncy Guida and

____

(your name)

What's your favorite way to travel?
Pick one, or make up your own.

by hot air balloon

by car

by camel

by magic carpet

by plane

by ____________________

Draw a picture of yourself starting out on a trip.

Write where you are going.

"I am going to ______________________."

Pick a word to write on the sign, or make up your own.

Then finish the picture.

DINOSAUR	KANGAROO
ELEPHANT	ALIEN

CAUTION:
CROSSING

You're going to the jungle!
What are you going to pack?

Make a list of things.

PACKING LIST

Draw them in the backpack.

Send your best friend a postcard from the jungle.

Draw the picture.

Fill in the message.

Things I like about riding in the car:

(Check which ones.)

____ Eating junk food

____ Stopping at rest stops

____ Singing along with my tapes at the top of my lungs

What else?

____

____

____

____

Things I DON'T like about riding in the car:

(Check which ones.)

____ Feeling sick from too much junk food

____ Trying to make my parents believe I really HAVE to go

____ Listening to my little brother's/sister's tapes

What else?

____

____

____

____

My Vacation in Outer Space

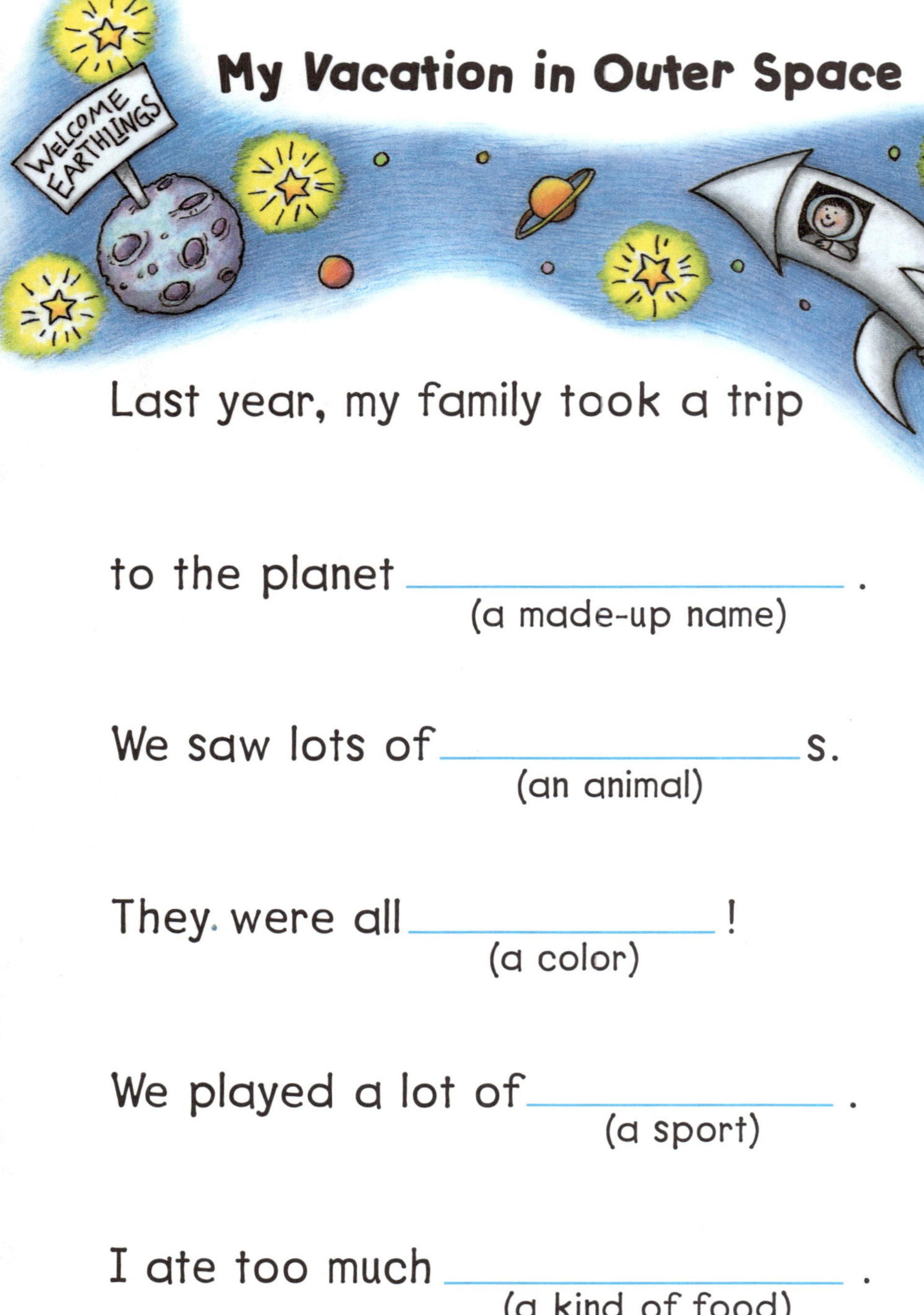

Last year, my family took a trip

to the planet ______________ .
(a made-up name)

We saw lots of ______________s.
(an animal)

They were all ______________ !
(a color)

We played a lot of ______________ .
(a sport)

I ate too much ______________ .
(a kind of food)

It was a ______________ vacation!
(a word that describes something)

Draw a picture of your trip.

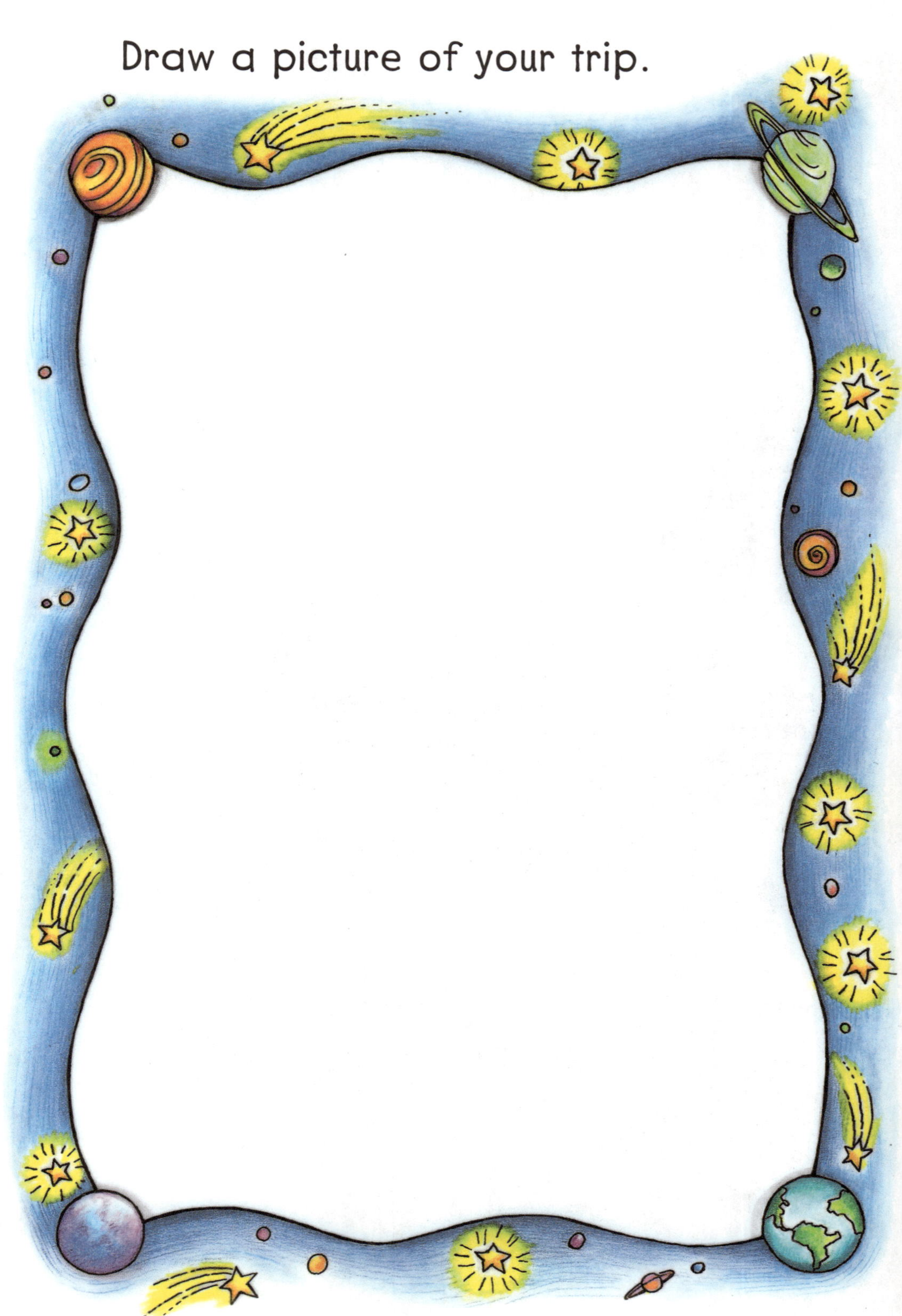

Pick a word to write on the sign, or make up your own.

Then finish the picture.

ROCKS
CHICKENS
PING-PONG BALLS
MEATBALLS

DANGER
FALLING

Welcome to the time machine!
Draw yourself now.

I am ____________ years old.

Draw yourself coming out as a grown-up.

I am ______________ years old.

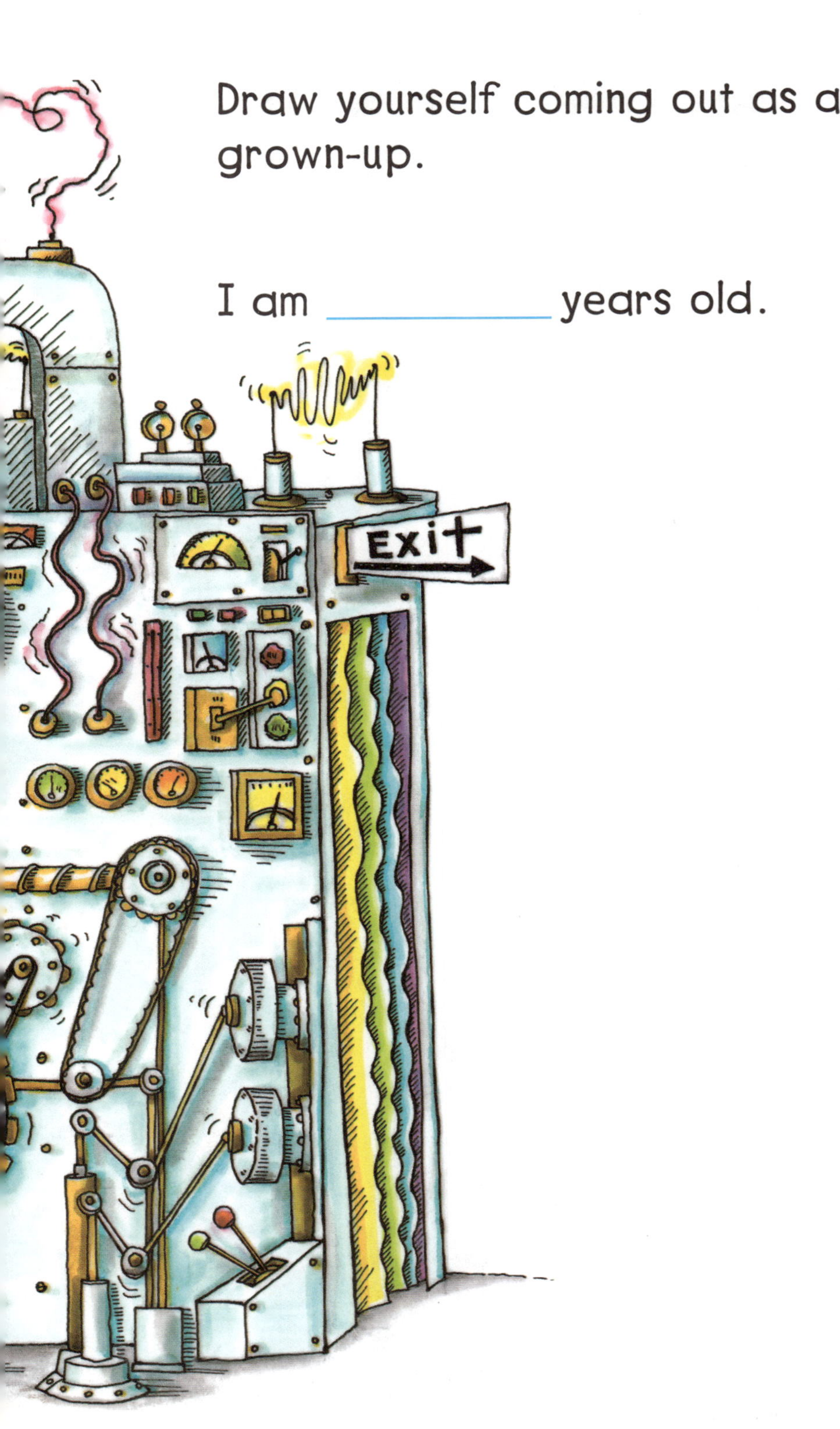

Draw a picture of a place that you like to visit.

Write words that describe it.

Draw a picture of a place that you DON'T like to visit.

Write words that describe it.

If you could choose where to go on your class field trip, where would you go?

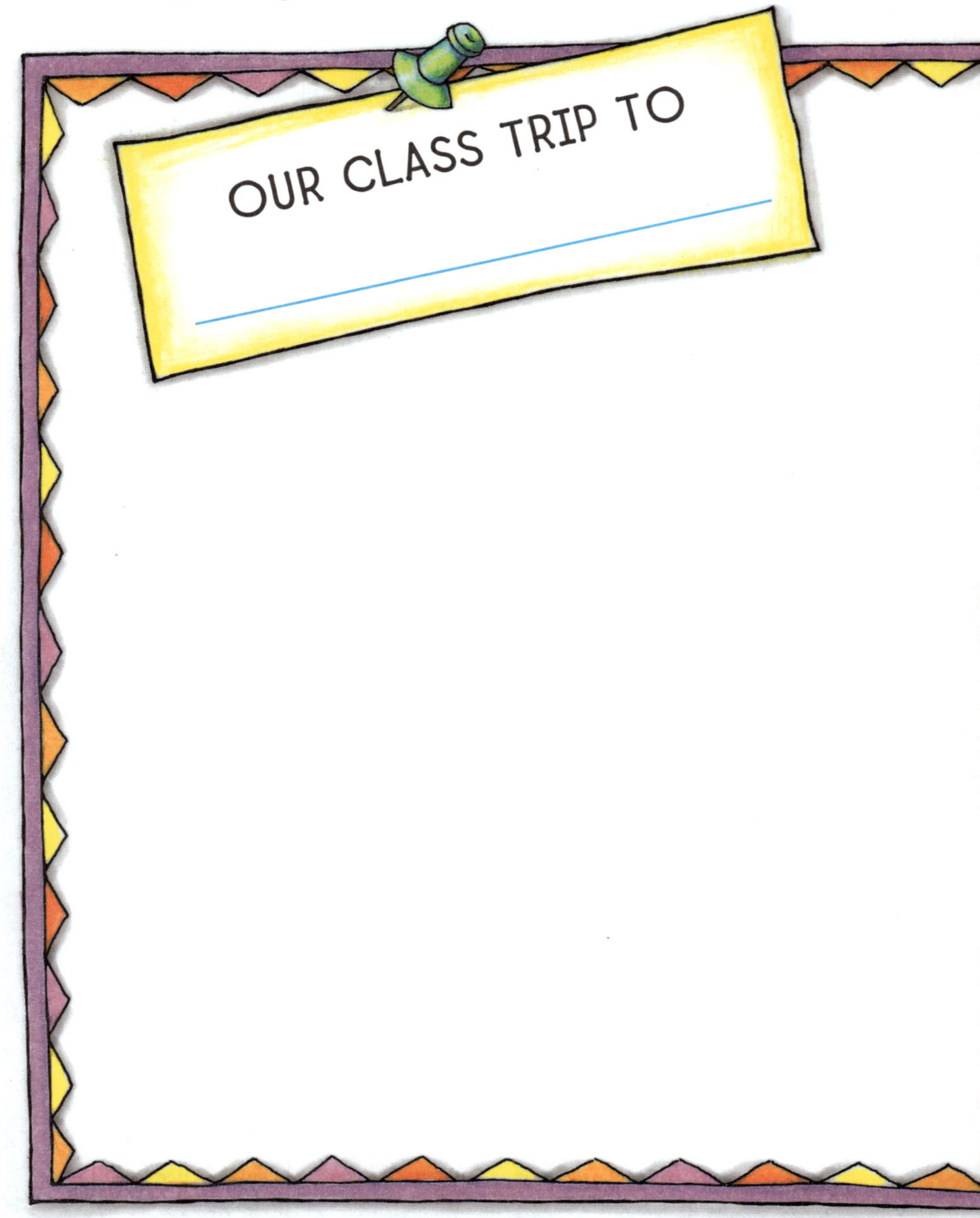

Draw a picture of you and your class on your field trip.

You're going to the South Pole! What are you going to pack? Make a list of things.

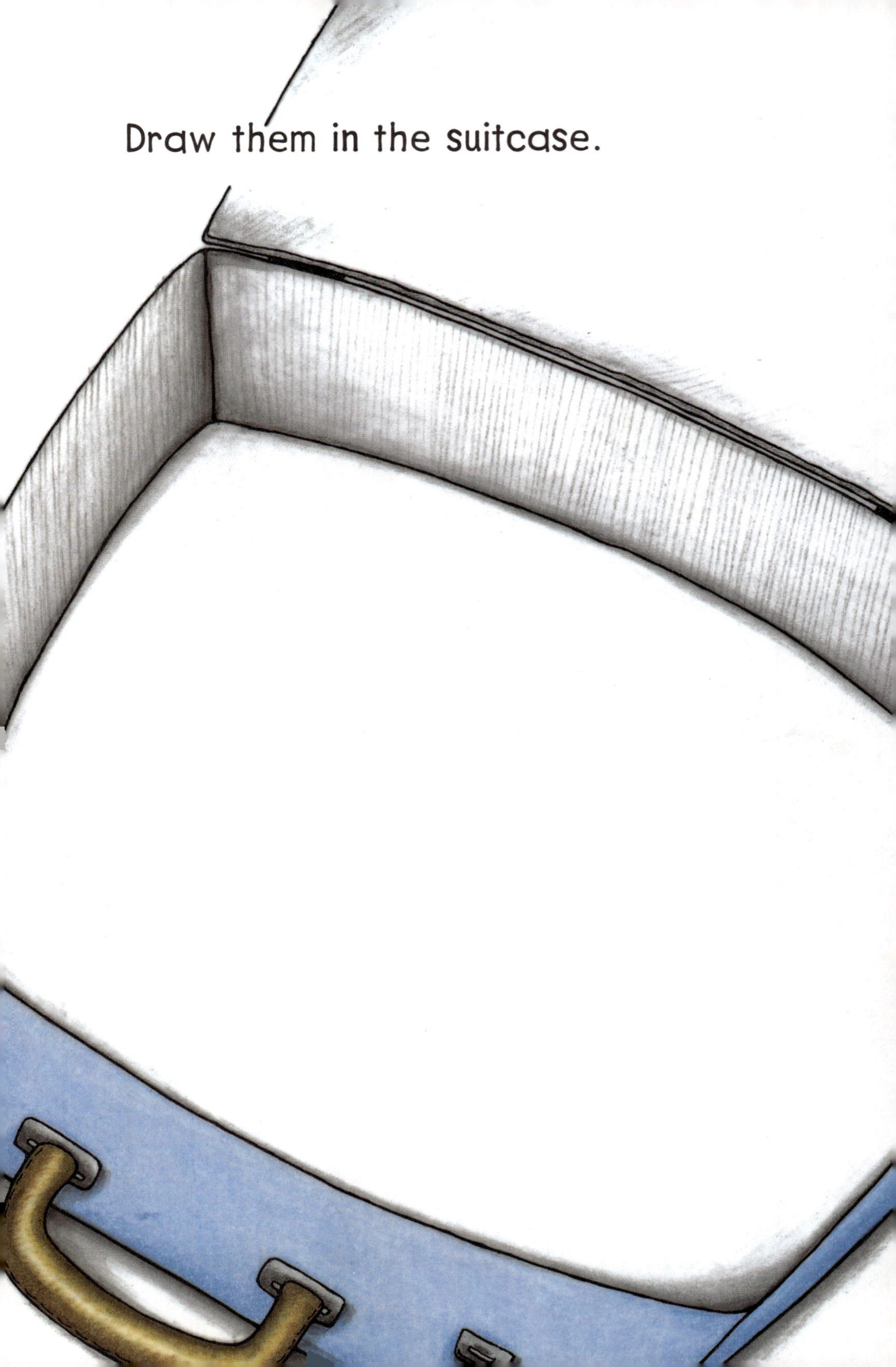
Draw them in the suitcase.

Send home some presents
from the South Pole.

Draw them in the boxes.
Fill out the tags.

AIR MAIL
To:
From:

You just invented a car that can drive, fly, and sail!

Draw it.

Oh, no!
You're stuck on a deserted island.
Good thing you brought...

Draw three things.
Label your pictures.

Pick a word to write in the cartoon, or make up your own. Then finish the picture.

ICEBERG
SHARKS
PIRATES
GIANT DUCKS

"
ahead!"

You just discovered a lost city! What did you dig up?

Draw something that starts with each letter of the alphabet. Label your pictures.

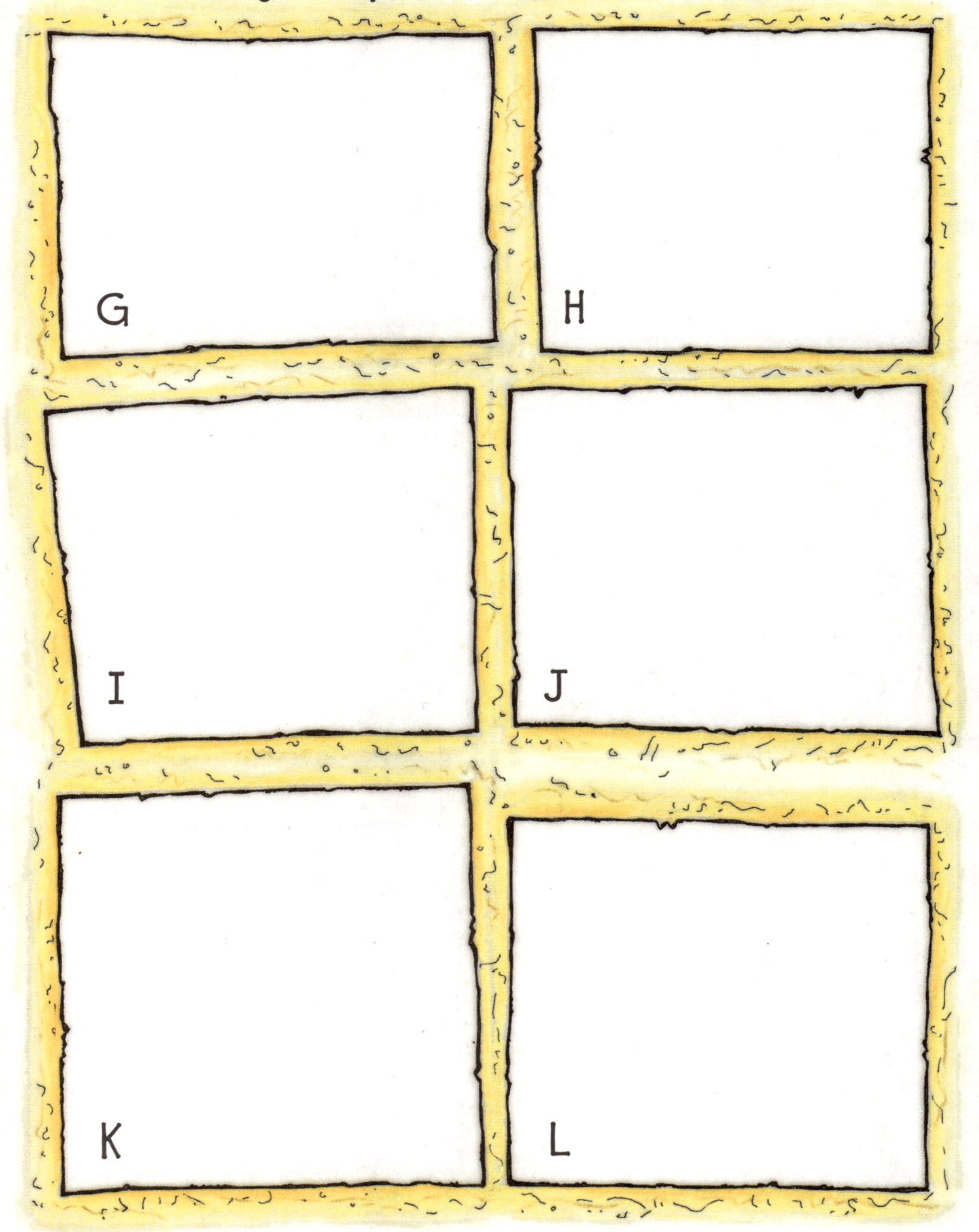

Keep digging!

S
T
U
V
W
X
Y
Z

What's causing the traffic jam?

Draw it in the picture.

Write words that describe it.

You're going to Mars!
What are you going
to pack?

Make a list of things.

PACKING LIST

____

____

____

____

____

Draw them in the bag.

Make a photo album with your pictures from Mars.

Finish the captions.
Then draw the pictures.

My spaceship,

the Mighty ______________________

My Martian friends, ______________,

______________, and me

______________________ Pizza,
our favorite Martian restaurant

Draw you and your family at home.